MEENA DIARIES

First Day Disaster at School

Written By
Sarika Hogade

Illustrated By
L. Roy tonmoy

Published in July 2021

ISBN: 978-1-7776716-0-0 (Paperback)

To,
Tvisha and Swadha

It was a beautiful Monday morning. Meena was still asleep in her bed. Her mother came in and said, "Good morning Meena! It is time to wake up. Today is your first day at kindergarten."

"What should I wear to school?"
asked Meena.

"When I do new things, I like to wear what I am most comfortable in," said Mom.
So Meena grabbed her favorite dress and got ready.

In school, Meena was new in the class.
"Hi, my name is Lane. I like your dress."
said Lane.
"Thank you, Lane! I am Meena.
I like your hair." said Meena.

Jim and Rob were putting away their backpacks next to the girls.

"What is she wearing?" asked Jim.

"I don't know", said Rob.

Meena heard their discussion and felt surprised that they were talking about her.

The lunch bell rang. Meena was so excited to eat food her mom had packed for her. It was her favorite 'daal rice'.
"What is that?" Lane asked Meena.
"It looks good!" said Celeste.

"What is that smell?" Jim asked from the other table holding his nose.
Meena heard it and felt a bit bad.
She said, "it's nothing." and closed her lunch box.

In the playground, Meena showed her twirls to Celeste.
"Wow! It looks beautiful when you twirl like that. I like those colors!" said Celeste.

"Hey, do you both want to play tag with me?" asked Rob.
"Okay," both agreed.
"My turn first," said Rob.
Rob chased after them both. He got close and tried to tag Meena.
But somehow he caught her dress. It made a huge ripping sound.

Meena felt angry. She thought that Rob ripped her favorite dress. “Did you do this on purpose because you didn’t like my dress earlier?” said Meena.

“Hey, why can’t you wear the dress like everyone else?” Rob replied.

When Meena's mom came to pick her up after school, Meena ran and hugged her. "I am so glad to see you Meena. How was your first day?" asked Mom. "I don't want to talk about it. Can we go home?" said Meena sadly.

Mom was worried so she asked, "Meena, you don't look happy. Did something upset you?" Meena explained everything.

"I am feeling sad and angry.
First, they talked about my dress.
At lunchtime, everyone was asking about my food. Later my dress got ripped at the playground. I think he did it on purpose." Meena started sobbing.

"It sounds like you
had a hard day,"
said Mom.
"I did," Meena
sniffled.

"It must be hard for your classmates as well, not knowing the things that you're doing. If you didn't know how to play with a new toy, you'd ask questions. That's what they were doing. I've got an idea for tomorrow." said mom.

“Now, about the dress, when accidents happen in school you can change your dress. I always give you extra clothes in your bag.

I will show you the trick on how to tie the knot when you play." said mom.

"Meena, I have an idea!"
Mom shared her idea
with Meena.
Then she sewed up the
rip in Meena's dress.

Next day Meena got to school.

Meena took few dresses from her bag.
"Would you like to try these dresses?" Meena asked her friends.
"I would love to," said Celeste. She took one dress and put it over the top of her dress.

Seeing Celeste wear the dress made the other girls want to do the same. They twirled circles in front of the classroom. The teacher came in and said, "You all look pretty in that dress".

During lunchtime,
Meena shared treats with the class.
"What is this, Meena?" Jim asked.
“Is it sweet or sour?” Rob asked.
Meena remembered her mom’s words.
“It’s Gulab jam,” Meena told everyone.
“It looks like a mini donut and tastes very sweet. I hope you all like it.
My mom made them.” said Meena.

“It tastes so good!” agreed Lane.
“Yummy!” said Jim.
Meena couldn’t stop grinning.

At playtime,
she tied her
dress
neatly around
her waist.
It won't get in
the way.

Meena said to Rob,
"This should do the trick."
Rob said, "Looks like it. It won't come in the way. Sorry about yesterday."
Meena said, "No problem! I am sorry for blaming you. It was an accident.
I understand it."

They both became friends.
Kids started playing together happily.

Everyone was looking at the sky.
Their hearts were open to each other.
Everyone felt happiness and pure joy.

Made in the USA
Middletown, DE
05 August 2021

45146704R00020